CORNERSTONES OF FREEDOM

HOMELAND SECURITY

BY ROBIN S. DOAK

CHILDREN'S PRESS®
An Imprint of Scholastic Inc.
New York Toronto London Auckland Sydney
Mexico City New Delhi Hong Kong
Danbury, Connecticut

BRINGING HISTORY to LIFE

Content Consultant
Christopher Gelpi, PhD
Professor of Political Science
Duke University
Durham, North Carolina

Library of Congress Cataloging-in-Publication Data

Doak, Robin S. (Robin Santos), 1963–
Homeland security/Robin S. Doak.
    p. cm.—(Cornerstones of freedom)
Includes bibliographical references and index.
  ISBN-13: 978-0-531-25036-5 (lib. bdg.) ISBN-10: 0-531-25036-9 (lib. bdg.)
  ISBN-13: 978-0-531-26561-1 (pbk.)   ISBN-10: 0-531-26561-7 (pbk.)
1. United States. Dept. of Homeland Security—Juvenile literature.
2. Terrorism—United States—Prevention—Juvenile literature. 3. National
Security—United States—Juvenile literature. I. Title. II. Series.
  HV6432.4.D63 2012
  363.340973—dc22   2011010750

Printed in the United States of America 113
SCHOLASTIC, CHILDREN'S PRESS, CORNERSTONES OF FREEDOM™,
and associated logos are trademarks and/or registered trademarks of
Scholastic Inc.

1 2 3 4 5 6 7 8 9 10 R 21 20 19 18 17 16 15 14 13 12

Photographs © 2012: Alamy Images: 15 (Todd Gipstein/National
Geographic Image Collection), 28 (Stephen Saks Photography); AP
Images: 4 top, 6 (Chao Soi Cheong), 20 (Brett Coomer, Houston Chronicle),
cover main, 8, 10, 13, 56, 58 (Charles Dharapak), 19 (Mel Evans), 39 (Ross
D. Franklin), 22 (Frank Franklin II), 35 (Haraz N. Ghanbari), 48 (David
Goldman), 34 (Mark Hertzberg, Journal Times), 12 (Carolyn Kaster), 7
(Doug Mills), 24, 29 (Denis Poroy), 36 (Nick Ut), 21, 51 (Ted S. Warren), 27
(Pat Wellenbach), 46 (Elizabeth Williams), 23 (Sam Yu, Frederick News
Post); FEMA News Photo/Jocelyn Augustino: 37; Getty Images: 40, 59
(Derick E. Hingle/Bloomberg), 2, 3, 30, 31 (Sandy Huffaker), 50 (David
McNew), 4 bottom, 54 (Mandel Ngan/AFP), 14 (Joshua Roberts/AFP);
Landov, LLC: 42, 44 (Hyungwon Kang/Reuters), back cover (Matthew
Staver); Media Bakery/GlowImages: 16; Robin Doak: 64; ShutterStock,
Inc./Mirek Kijewski: cover inset; U.S. Air Force/Senior Airman John
Hughel: 38; US Coast Guard: 5 bottom, 32, 41 (Petty Officer 2nd Class
Jonathen E. Davis), 55 (Petty Officer 3rd Class Casey J. Ranel), 18
(Illustration by Coast Guard artist Dino Sistilli), 26 (Petty Officer 3rd Class
David Weydert), 45, 57; Wikimedia Commons/Department of Homeland
Security: 5 top, 11.

Did you know that studying history can be fun?

BRING HISTORY TO LIFE by becoming a history investigator. Examine the evidence (primary and secondary source materials); cross-examine the people and witnesses. Take a look at what was happening at the time—but be careful! What happened years ago might suddenly become incredibly interesting and change the way you think!

Contents

4

SETTING THE SCENE

Freedom from Fear

The September 11, 2001, attacks were one of the most devastating events in U.S. history.

On September 11, 2001, a group of terrorists hijacked four airplanes and used them as weapons against the United States. They used the airplanes to attack the World Trade Center in New York City and the Pentagon in Washington, D.C. Nearly 3,000 people were dead by the end of the day as a result of the terrorists' actions.

Life changed that day for all Americans. Before September 11, many Americans believed that terrorist attacks were something that only happened in more troubled parts of the world. After 9/11, as the event came to be called, Americans were afraid. Could these attacks have been prevented? What could be done to stop future attacks?

The U.S. government acted quickly. On October 8, 2001, President George W. Bush created two temporary government agencies to focus on homeland security issues. Those two agencies became part of the new Department of Homeland Security (DHS) in early 2003. The DHS was established so that Americans could be safe and continue to enjoy freedom from fear.

President Bush (center) views the ruins of the World Trade Center in the aftermath of 9/11.

BOMBING KILLED SIX PEOPLE.

CHAPTER 1

THE HOMELAND SECURITY DEPARTMENT

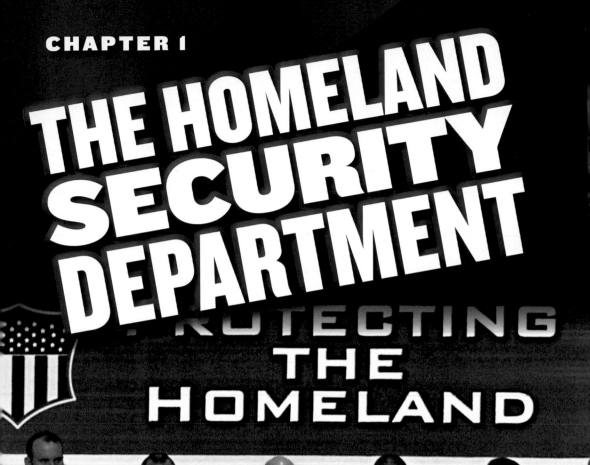

PROTECTING THE HOMELAND

President Bush speaks at a Homeland Security Department ceremony.

ON JANUARY 24, 2003, THE Department of Homeland Security became an active government agency. The overall goal of the DHS is to protect the nation from the many threats it faces. It is in charge of keeping Americans as safe as possible.

The DHS's mission covers five key areas. Its first goal is to prevent **terrorism** and strengthen security. Preventing terrorist attacks is the top priority of the DHS.

The DHS is also responsible for securing and managing the nation's borders. It protects the borders with Canada and Mexico. It also protects U.S. air and sea borders. Another related goal is to enforce and oversee immigration laws. The DHS is in charge of making sure that all the people in America have the legal right to be there.

President Bush signs a bill that provides the Department of Homeland Security with $30 billion to help protect America from terrorist threats.

The DHS is in charge of safeguarding and securing **cyberspace**. The department works to make sure that government and other high security computer information systems are protected. The DHS also makes sure the nation is prepared for emergencies and natural disasters such as hurricanes and floods.

A Massive Federal Agency

The DHS is headquartered in Washington, D.C. It is the third-largest department in the U.S. government. By March 1, 2003, 22 existing government agencies had been folded into the new department. Many of these agencies remained the same. But some, such as the Immigration and Naturalization Service, were reorganized. The DHS had 16 major departments by 2011. Each one was in charge of a different aspect of homeland security.

The DHS directly employs more than 230,000 people and has a yearly budget of $56 billion. The agency is headed by a secretary who oversees all of the departments'

SPOTLIGHT ON

Homeland Security Agencies

The creation of the DHS was the largest reorganization of government since 1947. When President Bush signed the Homeland Security Act into law, 22 existing federal agencies were reassigned to be part of the new department. These agencies included:

- U.S. Customs Service
- Immigration and Naturalization Service (INS)
- Transportation Security Administration (TSA)
- Federal Emergency Management Agency (FEMA)
- Federal Law Enforcement Training Center (FLETC)
- National Communications System (NCS)
- Nuclear Incident Response Team (NIRT)
- U.S. Coast Guard (USCG)
- U.S. Secret Service

President Obama meets with his cabinet in early 2011.

activities. This person is also the face of the DHS. The secretary meets the press and presents important information about homeland security to the public. The secretary is also a member of the president's **cabinet**. The cabinet advises the president on important issues.

The DHS also works with state and local agencies to help strengthen security in certain locations. The DHS works with more than 87,000 groups around the nation. One of the department's many important goals is to organize the exchange of information among all these agencies.

A New System for Terror Alerts

The DHS's most important goal is to prevent terrorist attacks in the United States. One of its first acts was to create a system for warning Americans about possible terrorist threats. It was a color-coded system known as the Homeland Security Advisory System (HSAS).

The HSAS measured terrorist threats in five levels: green, blue, yellow, orange, and red. A green threat level indicated a low risk of terrorism. A red threat indicated that the risk

SPOTLIGHT ON

Tom Ridge

Tom Ridge was the first secretary of Homeland Security. Ridge was a Vietnam War veteran and governor of Pennsylvania in 2001. President Bush chose Ridge to head up the newly created Homeland Security Office shortly after 9/11. He later took the top position when the DHS was founded. Ridge continued to run the DHS until his resignation in February 2005. He wrote a book after leaving office about his experiences in Washington. Ridge's book caused some controversy. It revealed that President Bush had asked Ridge to raise the terror alert level in 2004. This was done to help Bush get reelected.

of a terrorist attack was severe. But the HSAS gave no information about where the attack might take place or what type of threat was expected. Many people criticized the HSAS. It was eventually ignored by most Americans.

Tom Ridge explains the color-coded advisory system that was meant to help citizens prepare for potential terrorist attacks.

The DHS introduced a new warning system in January 2011 called the National Terrorism Advisory System. Information about specific and believable threats is passed on directly to the public under the

A FIRSTHAND LOOK AT
THE NATIONAL TERRORISM ADVISORY SYSTEM

The DHS introduced a new system in 2011 called the National Terrorism Advisory System to warn Americans about probable threats. The system includes announcements on TV and radio, as well as on the DHS Web page. See page 60 for a link to view the system's current status.

The color-coded threat condition system signs quickly became a common sight at U.S. airports.

new system. Such threats are sorted into either **elevated** or **imminent** categories.

The DHS makes public announcements when it receives information on threats. These announcements are made through the Internet, television, radio, and other means. The announcements include information on the threat. They also explain what the DHS is doing to make sure Americans are safe. They also tell Americans how to protect themselves. The threat warnings have specific end dates so that people know when threats are expected to be over. The new system began to be used in April 2011.

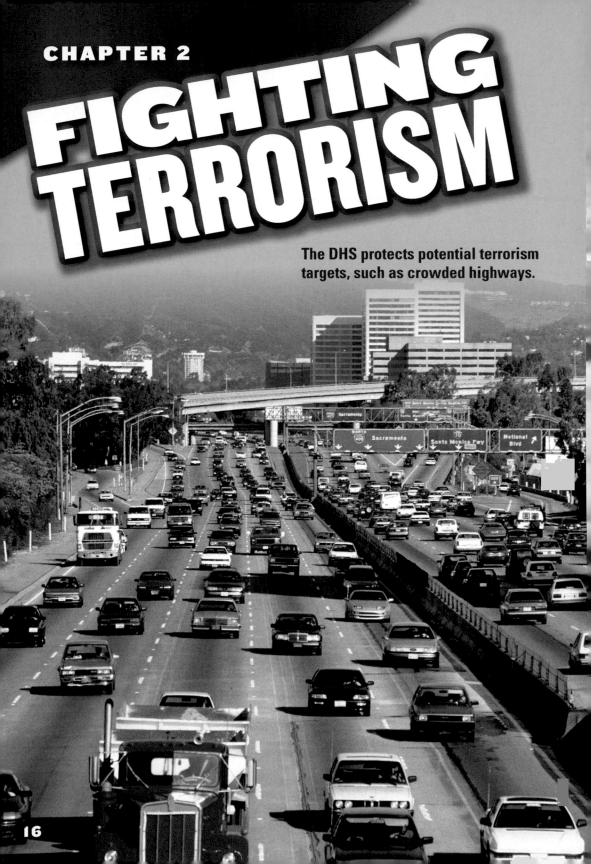

CHAPTER 2

FIGHTING TERRORISM

The DHS protects potential terrorism targets, such as crowded highways.

Preventing terrorism in

America is no simple task. Many **extremist** groups want to harm the United States. Most of these groups are headquartered in other countries. But some are in the United States as well.

These groups have a nearly limitless number of targets to choose from. There are millions of miles of bridges, tunnels, and superhighways. Military bases are also high-risk areas for such attacks. Groups of people gather daily on crowded city streets. They go to sporting and concert events and shopping malls. Other targets include natural gas wells, oil pipelines, financial institutions, and emergency systems. Even cyberspace could be targeted by terrorist groups.

Collecting Information

DHS collects information to help in the fight against terrorism. The department works with information services and intelligence agencies such as the Federal Bureau of Investigation (FBI) and the Central Intelligence Agency (CIA). They all gather and exchange data on possible terrorist activity. Agencies within the DHS monitor phone calls and e-mails of suspected terrorists. They may work with informants to reveal terrorist plots. Informants are people who give information on the activities of others. The agencies might also interview suspected terrorists who are already in prison. Agents in some departments may even act as spies to help expose terrorist activity.

Counterterrorism Departments

Certain DHS departments focus on fighting terrorism. The Transportation Security Administration (TSA) works to make sure terrorists do not attack places such as airports and railroads. The U.S. Coast Guard patrols the waters surrounding the country to prevent attacks by sea. The U.S. Customs and Border Protection department ensures that terrorists do not sneak in through the country's borders with neighboring countries. These departments work together to make it difficult for terrorists to launch attacks on U.S. soil.

New Jersey senator Frank Lautenberg answers questions from the public about the "If You See Something, Say Something" program.

The DHS also relies on the public for help fighting terrorism. It launched a national program in July 2010 that had been started in New York in 2002. It was called "If You See Something, Say Something." The program encourages people to report to local law enforcement any suspicious behavior they observe. The DHS has partnered with transportation companies, police departments, and department stores to bring its message to the public.

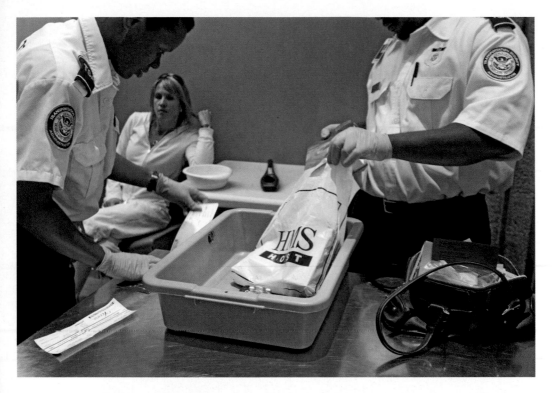

TSA agents perform baggage searches to make sure passengers do not bring dangerous items onto planes.

Security in the Air

Flying has become much safer in the past decade thanks to the DHS. The Transportation Security Administration (TSA) is a department within DHS that is in charge of airline safety. It is also in charge of other transportation systems such as trains and subways.

TSA workers patrol airports looking for bombs and suspicious activity. They screen passengers for dangerous items. They also travel on flights to prevent terrorism. The TSA also trains flight crews on how to defend against hijackers.

Protecting against Nuclear and Other Threats

The DHS protects the country against the threat of nuclear attack. The department works to stop terrorists who might build crude nuclear bombs out of stolen or illegal materials. Terrorists might also build explosive devices called dirty bombs that contain nuclear material.

The TSA scans all carry-on bags before they are allowed on planes.

Detectors scan cargo trucks for nuclear material as they leave a New York shipping terminal.

The Domestic Nuclear Detection Office (DNDO) is the branch of the DHS that is in charge of preventing nuclear attacks. Scientists at the DNDO work on detectors that help identify nuclear materials in cargo entering the United States. Some of these detectors can also be used on bridges, toll plazas, tunnels, and buildings.

The DHS also works to prevent biological and chemical attacks. Biological attacks might involve diseases such as **anthrax** that are spread on purpose throughout the population by terrorists. Anthrax is a disease caused by bacteria. It can lead to illness and death when breathed in. Chemical attacks are when toxic chemicals are spread in order to cause injury.

The Secret Service: Protecting the President

The Secret Service is another important DHS agency. It is in charge of protecting the president of the United States, the president's family, and other important government officials. Secret Service agents act as bodyguards and investigate threats.

The Secret Service also manages security for a National Special Security Event. Such events include the arrival of a visiting foreign president. In addition, the Secret Service oversees the nation's financial security. Agents investigate credit card fraud and other financial crimes.

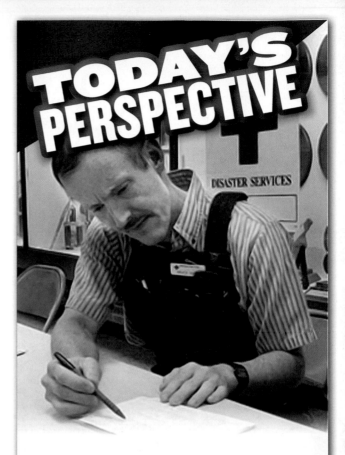

TODAY'S PERSPECTIVE

In 2001, someone sent anthrax to politicians and reporters through the mail. Five people who came into contact with the deadly virus died. Eleven others became seriously ill. In 2008, the FBI identified a scientist named Bruce Ivins (above) as the source of the attack. Ivins took his own life as the government was preparing to arrest him. The case was officially closed in 2010. But a 2011 report from the National Academy of Sciences raised questions about the way the FBI investigation was handled.

CHAPTER 3

BORDER SECURITY AND IMMIGRATION

The DHS keeps careful track of who crosses the U.S.-Mexico border.

PROTECTING THE NATION'S borders is an important part of keeping the United States secure. The United States shares a 4,000-mile (6,437 kilometer) border with Canada in the north. The southern border with Mexico is nearly 2,000 miles (3,219 km) long. The Department of Homeland Security makes sure that all people who cross these borders do so legally. The agency also prevents dangerous or illegal goods from being shipped or carried into the country.

The U.S. Coast Guard patrols the seas around the borders of the United States.

The Immigration and Naturalization Service was the only agency to police the borders before the DHS existed. That agency was split up into three separate departments in 2003. They are U.S. Citizenship and Immigration Services (USCIS), U.S. Immigration and Customs Enforcement (ICE), and U.S. Customs and Border Protection (CBP). The U.S. Coast Guard (USCG) polices the country's sea borders.

The USCIS oversees lawful immigration into the United States. Any person from another country who would like to work in the United States or become a U.S. citizen must apply to the USCIS. The department determines whether or not that person is eligible to come to this country. USCIS is also in charge of providing passports to American citizens who would like to travel to other countries.

ICE is in charge of investigating goods or people entering the United States illegally. It searches out drugs, weapons, and counterfeit goods, among other items. It looks for smugglers, **human traffickers**, and people who are living in the country illegally.

CBP officers patrol the land borders and screen all people and goods entering the United States. The CBP screens nearly a million people legally entering the

SPOTLIGHT ON

The Real ID Act

President Bush signed the Real ID (identification) Act into effect in 2005. The act requires all state driver's licenses and identification cards to meet minimum security standards. The new licenses must have special safety features that make them difficult to copy or alter. States must also now check original identification documents of all Americans renewing old licenses or getting new licenses. Each person's information will be recorded in a machine-readable area on the front of the new card. The goal of the act is to make it much more difficult for terrorists and criminals to obtain fake ID cards.

Many different types of vehicles and aircraft that have been used to patrol the U.S.-Mexico border are on display at the National Border Patrol Museum in Texas.

country each day. Department workers might arrest more than 2,000 criminals or people who are in the country illegally on the same day.

One of the department's most important programs is the Container Security Initiative. This program ensures

A FIRSTHAND LOOK AT
THE NATIONAL BORDER
PATROL MUSEUM

The National Border Patrol Museum offers visitors a look at the history of security along the U.S.-Mexico border, from the Old West to present day. See page 60 for a link to find out more about the museum and learn how you can visit it.

that cargo containers that enter the United States are carefully inspected so that no illegal weapon parts are shipped into the country. CBP officials use X-ray machines and radiation detection devices to check the containers.

Another important program is the Southwest Border Fence. The CBP is in the process of putting up more effective fences to block off 1,300 miles (2,092 km) of the U.S.-Mexico border. The fences would prevent vehicles and people from sneaking across the border unnoticed. The CBP also uses cameras and unmanned air vehicles called drones to scan the border.

The Southwest Border Fence adds extra protection to the original fence lying along the U.S.-Mexico border.

Drug Tunnels

Some Mexican drug lords are going underground to bring illegal drugs into the United States. They dig deep tunnels below the U.S.-Mexico border to avoid detection by the CBP. Officials have found more than 110 drug tunnels between Mexico and the United States since 2001. Many of these tunnels were between Nogales, Mexico, and Nogales, Arizona. Officials worry that the drug cartels might allow terrorist groups to use the tunnels to enter the United States.

Guarding U.S. Shores

The USCG prevents criminals and illegal goods from entering the United States by sea. The Coast Guard was part of the Department of Transportation before 2003. It is controlled by the U.S. Navy during times of war.

The Coast Guard patrols the waters in search of people smuggling illegal drugs, weapons, and other goods. It also keeps an eye out for other suspicious activity. Terrorists could use small boats to enter the country or launch weapons. Boats might even be packed with explosives and used as floating bombs to attack U.S. ships.

The USCG is in charge of enforcing laws relating to the sea and keeping the coastal waters safe for all boats and ships. It inspects vessels, lighthouses, buoys, and navigation systems to make sure the seas are safe. The USCG also conducts search and rescue missions on U.S. waters.

Other departments within DHS also contribute to border safety and immigration control. The TSA checks for illegal people and goods at airports. The Office of Intelligence and Analysis constantly studies information about all U.S. borders. It finds weaknesses and studies threats. It then passes this information on to other departments that need it.

A Homeland Security special agent crawls through a drug tunnel found near a warehouse on the U.S.-Mexico border.

CHAPTER 4

PREPARING FOR EMERGENCIES

The Department of Homeland Security assisted the Coast Guard during the cleanup of the Deepwater Horizon oil spill in 2010.

THE DHS IS ALSO IN CHARGE of preparing for and dealing with disasters. Such disasters could include terrorist attacks like the ones on 9/11. The DHS helps people before, during, and after natural disasters. These disasters might include hurricanes, blizzards, or floods. The agency also steps in after unexpected emergencies such as the Deepwater Horizon oil spill in 2010.

Prepared, Not Scared

The Federal Emergency Management Agency (FEMA) is in charge of emergency readiness. The agency's goal is to make sure that all Americans, especially **first responders**, are ready for any emergency.

FEMA is headquartered in Washington, D.C. But the agency has offices across the nation. FEMA partners with national, state, and local groups to keep the public up-to-date and well informed about potential disasters. The agency works with the Red Cross and the National Weather Service to spread information on possible threats.

Throughout the United States, volunteers are learning how to prepare for emergencies and disasters.

The DHS encourages all Americans to get involved and develop their own emergency plans. A DHS department called Citizen Corps offers training and online lectures. These teach people how to prepare for emergencies. The corps tells people what they can do to make sure that their families and communities are ready to react. It counts on volunteers from around the nation to step up when the worst happens.

SPOTLIGHT ON

Michael Chertoff

On February 15, 2005, Michael Chertoff became the second secretary of Homeland Security. Chertoff worked as a lawyer and a federal judge before taking the position. He helped write the USA Patriot Act in 2001. This act gave the government increased power to fight terrorism. Critics complained the act would lead to privacy abuses because it allowed searches of e-mail, telephone, financial, and medical records. Chertoff reorganized the DHS to make the agency more efficient. He focused on airline safety and strengthening the country's borders with Mexico and Canada during his four-year term.

The DHS also maintains the Ready program. This national advertising campaign is aimed at all Americans. The program's Web site, *www.ready.gov*, contains information for kids, adults, and businesses on how to prepare for many different types of disasters. It also contains information about ordering kits to help prepare for emergencies such as natural disasters.

Disaster Response

The DHS also responds to ongoing emergency situations around the nation. FEMA uses up-to-date technology to chart and follow weather events as they occur. It coordinates Urban Search and Rescue to find and locate victims of natural disasters and other emergencies. The Coast Guard sometimes plays a leading role in disaster response as well.

Criticism after the Hurricane Katrina disaster in 2005 has led FEMA to work toward better handling of disaster response. Hurricane Katrina was one of the most powerful storms in recorded history. It slammed into the Gulf Coast at the end of 2005 and eventually killed

Citizens in Los Angeles, California, participate in a terrorism readiness and response exercise.

FEMA workers search for residents after Hurricane Katrina devastated New Orleans in 2005.

more than 1,800 people. The worst damage occurred in New Orleans. More than 700,000 people were forced to abandon their homes. Damages along the coast totaled $75 billion.

The Coast Guard took an active role during the disaster. The USCG rescued 33,000 people from the flooded city using helicopters and boats. Rescue swimmers helped those caught in floodwaters or stranded on tops of roofs.

People in the region were not as happy with the rest of the federal government's response during the disaster. Many accused the DHS and FEMA of waiting too long

Secretary of Homeland Security Michael Chertoff talks to political leaders and the media in Portland, Oregon.

to take action. "We are not where we need to be in our ability to manage catastrophic events," Secretary of Homeland Security Michael Chertoff admitted later.

Congress passed the Post-Katrina Emergency Management Reform Act in October 2006 as a result of the disaster. The purpose of the act was to make FEMA more efficient and effective. The agency was reorganized. New positions, departments, and policies were added.

Cleaning Up Afterward

FEMA helps people recover and rebuild once a disaster is over. The agency maintains a database used to reunite people who have been separated from their families in disaster areas. It also offers financial help and other aid to people who need to rebuild their homes or find new places to live.

The DHS played an important role in recovery after another serious emergency in the spring of 2010. An oil rig called Deepwater Horizon exploded just 41 miles (66 km) off

the southeast coast of Louisiana on April 20. The rig had been drilling an oil well deep below the ocean's surface. Eleven people were killed in the explosion. Seventeen more were injured. The rig sank two days later. But even worse damage was still ahead.

A Coast Guard responder vehicle skims oil from the water's surface at the Deepwater Horizon spill.

Thousands of barrels of oil gushed into the ocean from a ruptured pipe under the Gulf Coast waters. Nearly 5 million barrels of oil had escaped into the water before the pipe was capped. It was the largest accidental marine oil spill in history.

A FIRSTHAND LOOK AT
THE DEEPWATER HORIZON OIL SPILL

The Deepwater Horizon oil spill was the worst oil spill disaster in U.S. history. The Coast Guard maintains a visual library containing pictures, videos, and maps of the spill and cleanup. See page 60 for a link to check out the visual library for yourself.

The Coast Guard led the federal cleanup effort after the disaster. Coast Guard personnel were the first on the scene after the explosion. They later used helicopters and boats to track the oil. They helped clean up by using special equipment to contain the oil and restore the waters, beaches, and islands that were affected. The USCG also issued safety warnings for area ports affected by the spill.

A Coast Guard crew prepares to bring an oil skimming system back on board their vessel.

CHAPTER 5

HIGH-TECH SECURITY

Homeland Security
personnel carefully
monitor cyberspace
communications
to protect the
United States from
cyberterrorism.

AMERICANS RELY ON COMPUTER systems every day in today's high-tech society. Computers control electricity and other energy systems. Financial, medical, and other personal information is stored in cyberspace. Local, state, and federal governments use computers and the Internet for everything from storing employee information to communicating with one another.

The offices of the National Cybersecurity and Communications Integration Center in Arlington, Virginia, buzz with activity.

Protecting against Cyberterrorism

Cyberterrorism is a growing concern. A serious cyberattack could shut down the nation's economic **infrastructure** by taking down the systems that allow banks, hospitals, power grids, and other important resources to function. President Barack Obama has said that cybersecurity is one of the most serious economic and national security challenges in the nation today.

DHS secretary Janet Napolitano launched the National Cybersecurity and Communications Integration Center (NCCIC) in 2009. The center's job is to protect the country from cyberterrorism. It is open 24 hours a day to take reports of threats and incidents that might affect the nation's most important information technology.

The DHS also works to keep businesses, the public, and state and local governments informed of possible threats. The department encourages all people to be aware of the risk of cyberattacks. Such attacks could be large or small. A large attack might mean U.S. electrical systems are shut down. A small attack might involve stealing a person's identity in order to get false U.S. documents. Such small attacks could eventually lead to larger ones.

SPOTLIGHT ON

Janet Napolitano

Janet Napolitano was appointed secretary of the DHS by President Barack Obama in 2009. Napolitano was born in New York City. She earned a law degree from the University of Virginia. She served as Arizona's first female attorney general from 1999 to 2003. She was the governor of Arizona from 2003 to 2009. There, she witnessed security issues along the U.S.-Mexico border firsthand. Napolitano gave the first-ever State of Homeland Security Address in January 2011. She reminded Americans that everyone shares responsibility for keeping the nation safe.

Spreading the Message of Hate

Thanks to tighter security, it is more difficult for terrorists to enter the United States today than it once was. Extremist groups are working harder to recruit people from Western Europe and the United States to perform violent acts. A man named Faisal Shahzad tried

Faisal Shahzad was arrested and sentenced for planning to blow up Times Square in New York City in 2010.

to blow up Times Square in New York in 2010. Shahzad had been living in the United States since 1997. He even became a U.S. citizen in 2009.

Terrorists use the Internet to recruit new members by spreading their message of hate and violence. Some groups create Web sites asking for money or new recruits. These sites contain anti-American messages intended to cause hostility and angry feelings against the country.

Such Web sites can be useful to the DHS. Security experts can watch them for chats, messages, and information that might reveal potential terrorist attacks. The department also uses this information to identify the methods terrorists are using to exploit defense weaknesses. In late 2010, extremists used the Internet to discuss ways to get dangerous items through airport security. The DHS was able to strengthen weaknesses in the airport security systems.

A VIEW FROM ABROAD

In 2011, many Americans were upset that the president might be given the power to use a "kill switch" to shut off the Internet during a cyberattack. Officials in China have long had complete control over the country's Internet service. Chinese officials routinely remove news stories and comments that criticize the government. A Chinese professor said, "Westerners tend to think that ... there should be limitations on the government's power, but in China it's different."

It is important for the department to pay attention to these Web sites, even if they seem insignificant. "The terrorist threat facing our country has evolved significantly in the last 10 years—and continues to evolve—so that, in some ways, the threat facing us is at its most heightened state since those attacks [of 9/11]," says Janet Napolitano.

CHAPTER 6

HOMELAND SECURITY AND CIVIL RIGHTS

The Department of Homeland Security has been accused of watching lawful demonstrations in the United States too closely.

THE DEPARTMENT OF HOMELAND

Security was created to keep America safe from terrorism and protect Americans' freedom from fear. But some say that the agency goes too far. Critics accuse the DHS of being overly secretive and of violating **civil rights**.

Some critics take issue with the Real ID Act. They believe the program could lead to the government having unnecessary information about each U.S. citizen. Others accuse the DHS of illegally spying on U.S. citizens through Internet watches and computer searches. The American Civil Liberties Union claims that the DHS has been closely watching lawful protests and has targeted peaceful political groups. Some civil liberties groups have even sued the DHS to gain information on violations in airports and at U.S. border stations.

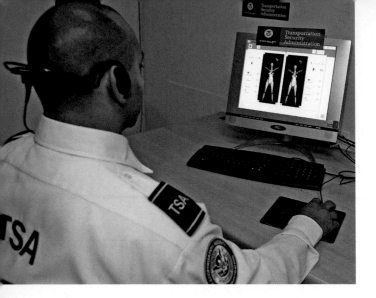

A Revealing Machine

The TSA began using high-powered full-body scanners at the end of 2010 to make sure air passengers were not carrying dangerous goods. The scanners use X-ray

A TSA screener views a passenger's image captured on a full-body X-ray scanner.

technology to see through clothes and detect bombs, weapons, and other banned items. Some people praised the new and improved scanners. But others complained that the machines violated their right to privacy. The Electronic Privacy Information Center, a public interest research center, called the machines "invasive, ineffective, and unconstitutional."

The scanner controversy highlighted a serious issue that the DHS deals with every day. How can the department best protect the United States without violating civil rights and civil liberties? Which is more important: freedom from fear or a right to privacy? These questions are not easily answered.

Responding to Criticism

The DHS has made efforts to ensure that people's civil rights and civil liberties are protected. The mission of the Office for Civil Rights and Civil Liberties (CRCL) is to protect the nation from threats "while preserving individual liberty, fairness, and equality under the law." CRCL handles complaints against the DHS and works to make sure that department workers understand people's concerns.

CRCL also works with groups that may be affected by DHS policies and programs. CRCL has met with Muslim, Arab, and Southeast Asian communities around the country to discuss homeland security and civil rights. It has encouraged these communities to partner with the agency in the fight to keep America safe.

YESTERDAY'S HEADLINES

Consumer advocate Ralph Nader spoke out in 2010 about the TSA security measures. In an editorial for *USA Today*, he wrote: "This month Homeland Security has implemented a new rule calling for extremely invasive pat-downs of commercial airline passengers who decline to use full-body, 'backscatter technology' scanners that use low-level X-rays. Pregnant women, parents with young children, adherents of religions, amputees and people with wireless insulin pumps or embedded medical devices are increasingly saying, 'No thanks.' They do not believe they should be exposed to technology that could pose risks, may malfunction, and certainly invades their privacy. So Homeland Security has doubled its trouble by turning to the invasive pat-downs. What the department should do is reconsider its use of these scanners."

What Happened Where?

MS

AL

LA

Mobile

Biloxi

New Orleans

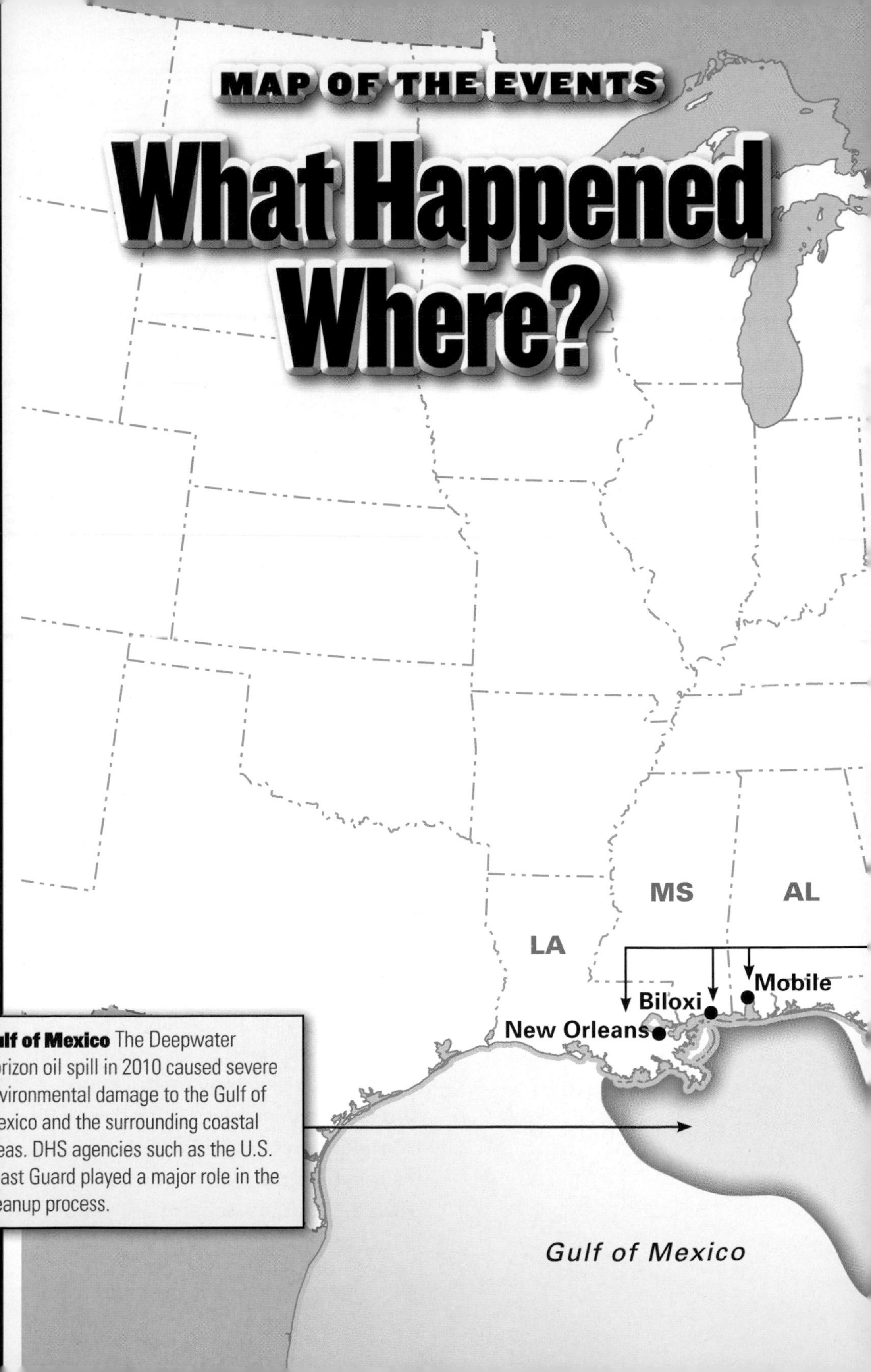

Gulf of Mexico The Deepwater Horizon oil spill in 2010 caused severe environmental damage to the Gulf of Mexico and the surrounding coastal areas. DHS agencies such as the U.S. Coast Guard played a major role in the cleanup process.

Gulf of Mexico

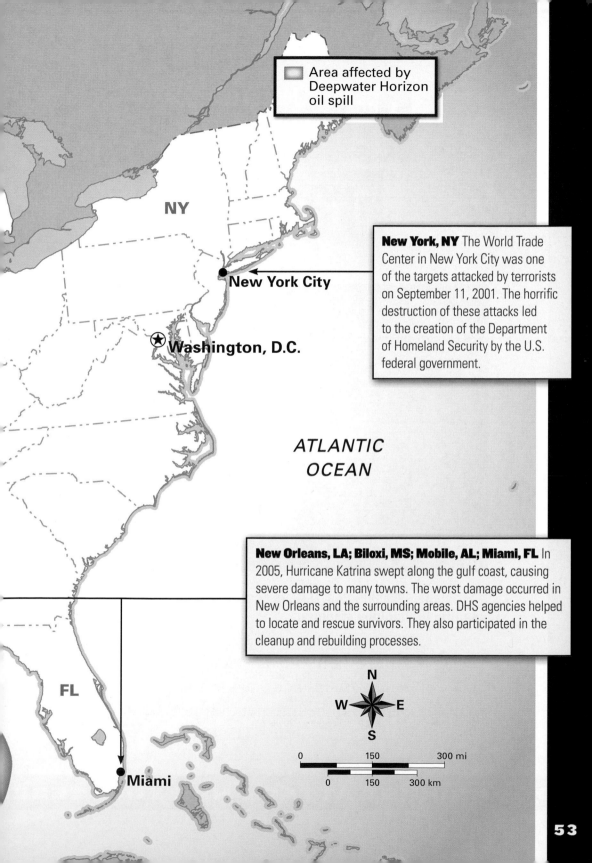

Area affected by Deepwater Horizon oil spill

NY

New York City

⭐ **Washington, D.C.**

New York, NY The World Trade Center in New York City was one of the targets attacked by terrorists on September 11, 2001. The horrific destruction of these attacks led to the creation of the Department of Homeland Security by the U.S. federal government.

ATLANTIC OCEAN

New Orleans, LA; Biloxi, MS; Mobile, AL; Miami, FL In 2005, Hurricane Katrina swept along the gulf coast, causing severe damage to many towns. The worst damage occurred in New Orleans and the surrounding areas. DHS agencies helped to locate and rescue survivors. They also participated in the cleanup and rebuilding processes.

FL

N
W E
S

0   150   300 mi
0   150   300 km

Miami

Preserving Freedom

A woman in Washington, D.C., is scanned in an advanced imaging technology machine.

The fight to preserve freedom from fear is an ongoing battle. Extremist groups find ways to reach new audiences. They use the Internet to spread their messages of hate and violence. The DHS and other

NO TERRORIST ATTACK HAS SUCCEEDE

groups must work harder to identify people already living in the United States who are influenced by such messages.

The DHS has made great strides since 2003. But the threat to the nation is not lessening. Janet Napolitano reported in February 2011 that the United States was at greater risk than it had been at any time since September 11, 2001. She urged the public to work with federal, state, and local agencies to pool information that might prevent a future attack.

"We cannot guarantee that there will never be another terrorist attack, and we cannot seal our country under a glass dome," said Napolitano. "However, we continue to do everything we can to reduce the risk of terrorism in our nation."

Janet Napolitano meets with members of the Coast Guard to discuss emergency relief plans.

IN THE UNITED STATES SINCE 9/11.

INFLUENTIAL INDIVIDUALS

Ralph Nader (1934–) is a lawyer, consumer advocate, and four-time presidential candidate. In 1965, his book *Unsafe At Any Speed* helped improve vehicle safety laws in the United States.

Tom Ridge (1945–) is a politician who served as the first secretary of Homeland Security from 2003 to 2005. He has also served as governor of Pennsylvania.

George W. Bush (1946–) was the 43rd president of the United States. He served from 2001 to 2009. He was president during the September 11 terrorist attacks and the beginning of the Iraq War.

George W. Bush

Michael Chertoff (1953–)
is an American lawyer and
businessman who served as the
secretary of Homeland Security
from 2005 to 2009. He has also
served as a federal judge.

Janet Napolitano (1957–)
was named secretary of
Homeland Security in 2009. She
formerly served as attorney
general and governor of Arizona.

Janet Napolitano

TIMELINE

| 2001 | 2002 | 2003 | 2005 |

September 11
Terrorists attack the World Trade Center in New York and the Pentagon in Washington, D.C. Another plane is crashed in Pennsylvania before reaching its unknown target.

September 18
Anthrax attacks through the U.S. mail cause the deaths of five people and make 11 others seriously ill.

October 8
President George W. Bush creates two temporary agencies to focus on homeland security.

November 25
President Bush signs the Homeland Security Act into law.

January 24
The Department of Homeland Security is established by an act of Congress.

March 1
All 22 existing federal agencies are merged under the DHS.

May 11
President Bush signs the Real ID Act into law.

August 29
Hurricane Katrina slams into the Gulf Coast, causing more than 1,800 deaths and billions of dollars in damage.

PROTECTING THE HOMELAND

2006

October
Congress passes the Post-Katrina Emergency Management Reform Act.

2009

January 21
Former Arizona governor Janet Napolitano is sworn in as the third secretary of the DHS.

2010

April 20
The oil rig Deepwater Horizon explodes, beginning a three-month-long oil spill.

July
The DHS launches the "If You See Something, Say Something" program.

2011

January
The DHS introduces a new warning system called the National Terrorism Advisory System.

LIVING HISTORY

Primary sources provide firsthand evidence about a topic. Witnesses to a historical event create primary sources. They include autobiographies, newspaper reports of the time, oral histories, photographs, and memoirs. A secondary source analyzes primary sources, and is one step or more removed from the event. Secondary sources include textbooks, encyclopedias, and commentaries.

Many primary source documents concerning the founding and organization of the DHS can be found at the Department of Homeland Security's Web site. For more information, visit *www.dhs.gov /xabout/history*

Deepwater Horizon Response from the U.S. Coast Guard
The U.S. Coast Guard's Web site contains information and photos documenting the Deepwater Horizon oil spill. You can see it all by visiting *http://cgvi.uscg.mil/media/main.php?g2_itemId=841811*

The Homeland Security Act of 2002
The Homeland Security Act marked the official creation of the Department of Homeland Security. You can read a copy online by visiting *www.dhs.gov /xlibrary/assets/hr_5005_enr.pdf*

National Border Patrol Museum
The National Border Patrol Museum in El Paso, Texas, offers artifacts and exhibits from the agency's history. Find out more by visiting *www. borderpatrolmuseum.com*

National Terrorism Advisory System (NTAS)
The DHS created the NTAS to replace the highly criticized Homeland Security Advisory System. You can check for terrorism alerts by visiting *www. dhs.gov/files/programs/ntas.shtm*

RESOURCES

Books

Ambrosek, Renee. *United States Policy on Immigration*. New York: Rosen Central, 2007.

Beyer, Mark. *Homeland Security and Weapons of Mass Destruction: How Prepared Are We?* New York: Rosen Publishing Group, 2005.

Campbell, Geoffrey. *A Vulnerable America: An Overview of National Security*. San Diego: Lucent, 2007.

Gaines, Ann. *Border Patrol Agent and Careers in Border Protection*. Berkeley Heights, NJ: Enslow Publishers, 2006.

Goldish, Meish. *Coast Guard: Civilian to Guardian*. New York: Bearport Publishing, 2011.

Kowalski, Kathiann M. *A Pro/Con Look at Homeland Security: Safety vs. Liberty after 9/11*. Berkeley Heights, NJ: Enslow Publishers, 2008.

Santella, Andrew. *September 11, 2001*. New York: Children's Press, 2007.

Souter, Gerry. *Secret Service Agent and Careers in Federal Protection*. Berkeley Heights, NJ: Enslow Publishers, 2006.

Web Sites

Ready
www.ready.gov
Explore this DHS site to learn about the program that helps Americans prepare for emergency situations.

United States Coast Guard
www.uscg.mil
Find out more about the Coast Guard.

U.S. Department of Homeland Security
www.dhs.gov
Learn more about the different agencies and the history of the DHS.

GLOSSARY

anthrax (AN-thraks) a disease caused by bacteria that can lead to illness and death when inhaled

cabinet (KAB-uh-nit) a group of high-ranking government officials who advise the president on important issues

civil rights (SIV-uhl RITES) rights that are guaranteed to all Americans by the U.S. Constitution, including freedom of speech and religion

cyberspace (SY-bur-spays) the virtual space in which computers communicate and operate over the Internet

cyberterrorism (sy-bur-TARE-ur-iz-uhm) terrorist attacks on computer and information systems

elevated (EL-uh-vay-tid) increased, as in an increased risk of terrorist threat

extremist (ek-STREE-must) someone who holds radical views or promotes radical actions

first responders (FURST ruh-SPON-durz) the emergency medical workers who are the first people to arrive in the event of a disaster

human traffickers (HYOO-muhn TRAF-ik-urz) people who bring other people to another country and force them to work against their will

imminent (IM-uh-nuhnt) ready to occur

infrastructure (IN-fruh-struk-chur) the underlying systems that allow something to function

terrorism (TARE-ur-iz-uhm) the use of violence and threats to spread fear and make political statements

INDEX

Page numbers in *italics* indicate illustrations.

ABOUT THE AUTHOR

Robin Doak has a bachelor's degree in English from the University of Connecticut. She has been writing for children for more than 20 years.